I0167378

Wisconsin Bingo Book

COMPLETE BINGO GAME IN A BOOK

WISCONSIN

FORWARD

E PLURIBUS UNUM

1848

Written By Rebecca Stark

ISBN 978-0-87386-542-5

Educational Books 'n' Bingo

Printed in the U.S.A.

DIRECTIONS

INCLUDED:

List of Terms

Templates for Additional Terms and Clues

2 Clues per Term

30 Unique Bingo Cards

Markers

1. **Either cut apart the book or make copies of ALL the sheets. You might want to make an extra copy of the clue sheets to use for introduction and review. Keep the sheets in an envelope for easy reuse.**

2. Cut apart the call cards with terms and clues.

3. Pass out one bingo card per student. There are enough for a class of 30.

4. Pass out markers. You may cut apart the markers included in this book or use any other small items of your choice.

5. Decide whether or not you will require the entire card to be filled. Requiring the entire card to be filled provides a better review. However, if you have a short time to fill, you may prefer to have them do the just the border or some other format. Tell the class before you begin what is required.

6. There are 50 terms. Read the list before you begin. If there are any terms that have not been covered in class, you may want to read to the students the term and clues before you begin.

7. There is a blank space in the middle of each card. You can instruct the students to use it as a free space or you can write in answers to cover terms not included. Of course, in this case you would create your own clues. (Templates provided.)

8. Shuffle the cards and place them in a pile. Two or three clues are provided for each term. If you plan to play the game with the same group more than once, you might want to choose a different clue for each game. If not, you may choose to use more than one clue.

9. Be sure to keep the cards you have used for the present game in a separate pile. When a student calls, "Bingo," he or she will have to verify that the correct answers are on his or her card AND that the markers were placed in response to the proper questions. Pull out the cards that are on the student's card keeping them in the order they were used in the game. Read each clue as it was given and ask the student to identify the correct answer from his or her card.

10. If the student has the correct answers on the card AND has shown that they were marked in response to the *correct questions,* then that student is the winner and the game is over. If the student does not have the correct answers on the card OR he or she marked the answers in response to *the wrong questions,* then the game continues until there is a proper winner.

11. If you want to play again, reshuffle the cards and begin again.

Have fun!

TERMS INCLUDED

American Water Spaniel

Badger

Joseph Bailey

Black Hawk

Border (-ed)

Central Plain

Climate

Coat of Arms

Crop(s)

Counties

Dairy

Eastern Ridges and Lowlands

Executive Branch

Flag

French and Indian War

Fruit

Fur Trade

Galena

Green Bay

Honeybee

Judicial Branch

Lake Michigan

Lake Superior

Lake Winnebago

Lead

Legislative Branch

Logging

Madison

Marquette and Joliet

Milk

Milwaukee

Mississippi River

Motto

Mourning Dove

Muskellunge

Jean Nicolet

Northwest Territory

Northern Highland

Paper

Polka

Red Granite

Song

Timms Hill

Tribes

Union

War of 1812

Western Upland

Wisconsin River

Wisconsin Territory

Frank Lloyd Wright

Additional Terms

Choose as many additional terms as you would like and write them in the squares. Repeat each as desired.
Cut out the squares and randomly distribute them to the class.
Instruct the students to place their square on the center space of their card.

Clues for
Additional Terms

Write two clues for each of your additional terms.

1. 2.	1. 2.
1. 2.	1. 2.
1. 2.	1. 2.

© Barbara M. Peller

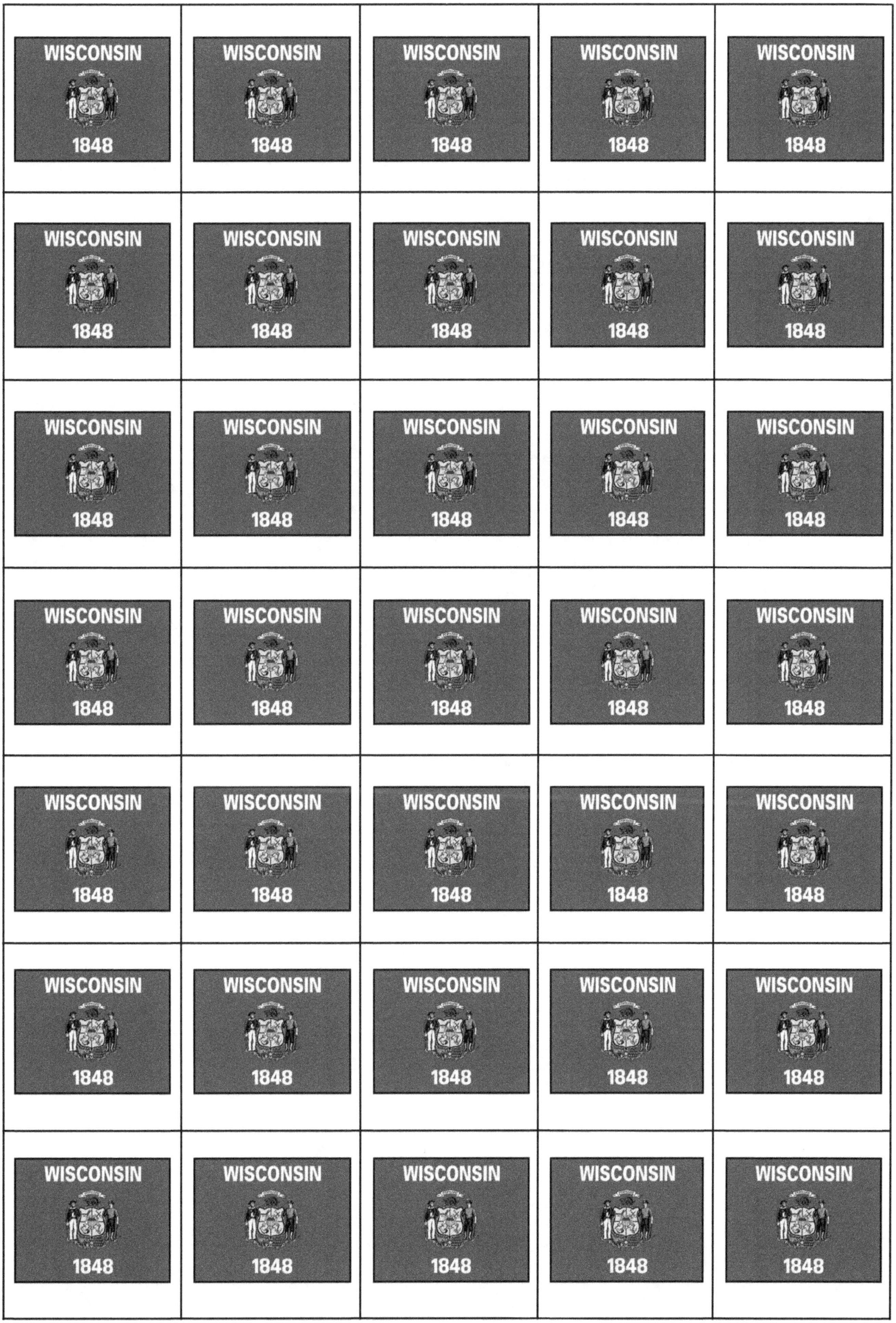

American Water Spaniel 1. The ___ is the state dog. 2. The ___ was chosen as the state dog because it is the only breed that is native to Wisconsin.	**Badger** 1. The ___ is the official state animal. The white-tail deer is the state wildlife animal. 2. Wisconsin's official nickname is the "___ State." It originally referred to the lead miners who lived in temporary caves cut into the hillsides.
Joseph Bailey 1. Wisconsin lumberman ___ is called the "Hero of the Red River." 2. During the Civil War, ___ had the idea to free the Union fleet by building dams similar to those used by Wisconsin River lumbermen to raise the water level when logs were stuck on rapids.	**Black Hawk** 1. The ___ War of 1832 started when members of the Sac, Fox, and Kickapoo tribes, led by Chief ___, attempted to resettle in their homeland. 2. The ___ War ended with the Bad Axe Massacre.
Border (-ed) 1. Minnesota, Michigan, Illinois, and Iowa ___ Wisconsin. 2. Wisconsin is ___ by Lake Michigan and Lake Superior.	**Central Plain** 1. The ___ is south of the Northern Highland. It curves across the central part of the state. 2. The ___ region is an area of buttes and mesas. In the southern portion, the Wisconsin River has carved a scenic gorge, known as the Wisconsin Dells.
Climate 1. Wisconsin has a continental ___, with cold, snowy winters and warm summers. 2. Lake Michigan and Lake Superior have an effect upon Wisconsin's ___.	**Coat of Arms** 1. The state ___ includes representations of Wisconsin's main industries: agriculture, mining, manufacturing, and navigation. The cornucopia and pile of lead represent farm products and minerals. 2. The ___ is the main feature of the state seal and the state flag.
Crop(s) 1. Corn, greenhouse and nursery products, soybeans, potatoes, snap beans, and cranberries are important ___. 2. The most important ___ is corn, which is used to feed the cattle. It is the state grain.	**Counties** 1. There are 72 ___ in Wisconsin. 2. ___ in Wisconsin are run by boards, headed by a chairperson. Those with a population of 500,000 or more have an executive as well.

© Barbara M. Peller

Dairy 1. ___ products; beef cattle and calves; hogs; broilers, or young chickens; and chicken eggs are important livestock products. 2. ___ products account for more than half of Wisconsin's total agricultural receipts. The ___ cow is the state domesticated animal and milk is the official state beverage.	**Eastern Ridges and Lowlands** 1. East of the Central Plain lie the gently rolling hills of the ___. This area extends from Green Bay south to Illinois. 2. The ___ area is the richest agricultural region of Wisconsin. Many of the largest cities in the state are in this region.
Executive Branch 1. The ___ of government enacts and enforces the laws. The governor, the lieutenant governor, the secretary of state, the state treasurer, the attorney general, and the state superintendent of public instruction are part of this branch. 2. The governor is head of the ___. The present-day governor is [fill in].	**Flag** 1. The state ___ has a dark blue field. The state coat of arms is centered on that field. 2. The word "Wisconsin" is in white letters at the top of the state ___.The date "1848" is on the bottom.
French and Indian War 1. The name of this conflict refers to the two main enemies of the colonists: the royal French forces and their Native allies. 2. The Treaty of Paris ended the ___. The British took control of the lands that had been claimed by France, including what is now Wisconsin.	**Fruit** 1. Cranberries, apples, and strawberries are leading ___ crops. 2. The cranberry is the state ___.
Fur Trade 1. French colonists were interested primarily in the ___. The first white settlement at Milwaukee was a tiny ___ post started in 1795 by Jacques Vieau. 2. Overhunting in Wisconsin Territory gradually caused the ___ to shift farther west.	**Galena** 1. ___ is the state mineral. It is the most common mineral that contains lead. 2. ___, or lead ore, was chosen as the state mineral because of its role in Wisconsin's history and economy.
Green Bay 1. Both the city and the bay were named for the color of the water. With the growth of railroads in the 1870s, ___ became a center of iron smelting, lumber milling, and paper products. 2. ___ is the home of the ___ Packers, a NFL franchise founded in 1919.	**Honeybee** 1. The ___ is the state insect. 2. Wisconsin is one of 17 states to have the ___ as an official symbol. Wisconsin produced around 3.6 million pounds of honey in 2011.

Wisconsin Bingo

Judicial Branch 1. The ___ interprets what our laws mean and makes decisions about the laws and those who break them. 2. The Supreme Court is the highest court in the ___ of the state government.	**Lake Michigan** 1. Wisconsin borders two of the 5 Great Lakes: ___ and Lake Superior. 2. Milwaukee, Green Bay, Sheboygan, Kenosha, and Racine are among the cities located on this lake.
Lake Superior 1. The ___ Lowland is a small area of flat plain in northern Wisconsin. It occupies parts of Douglas, Bayfield, and Ashland counties in the northwestern corner of the state. 2. ___ is the largest of the Great Lakes.	**Lake Winnebago** 1. ___ is the largest lake that is entirely within the state. 2. Cities on the shore of ___ include Oshkosh, Fond du Lac, Neenah, and Menasha.
Lead 1. There was a ___-mining boom in southwest Wisconsin and northwest Illinois. Many immigrants, including expert miners from Cornwall, England, were drawn to the region. 2. By the 1840s, southwest Wisconsin mines were producing more than half of the nation's ___.	**Legislative Branch** 1. The ___ of government comprises the Senate and the Assembly. 2. The ___ makes the laws.
Logging 1. From 1890 to 1910 ___ and forest products led Wisconsin's developing industrial economy. 2. Forests in 3 main regions were exploited for ___: the Wisconsin River Valley in the center of the state, the Wolf River in the northeast, and the watersheds of the Black and Chippewa rivers in the northwest.	**Madison** 1. ___ is the capital of Wisconsin. 2. The state's largest university campus is in ___ along the southern shore of Lake Mendota.
Marquette and Joliet 1. This team comprised a Jesuit missionary and a fur trader. They were the first Europeans to explore and map much of the Mississippi River. 2. In 1673 ___ explored the unsettled territory from the Lake Michigan region to the Gulf of Mexico for France. Wisconsin Bingo	**Milk** 1. ___ is the official state beverage. 2. ___ was adopted as the state beverage because Wisconsin is the leading producer of this product and because of its contribution to the state's economy.

Milwaukee
1. ___ is the largest city in Wisconsin. It is on the southwestern shore of Lake Michigan.
2. By 1860, there were almost 200 breweries in Wisconsin, more than 40 of them in___.This was due, in part, to the many German   immigrants in the 1840s and 1850s.

Mississippi River
1. The ___ forms part of the state's western border with Minnesota and Iowa.
2. Prairie du Chien is the oldest European settlement on the Upper Mississippi River. It is located just above the confluence of the ___ and the Wisconsin River.

Motto
1. The official state ___ is "Forward."
2. The state ___, "Forward," is on the state coat of arms and on the state quarter.

Mourning Dove
1. The ___ is the official state symbol of peace.
2. Two birds are official state symbols: the American robin, which is the state bird, and the ___, which is the symbol of peace.

Muskellunge
1. The ___, or musky, is the official state fish.
2. The ___ was the source of many "monster fish" stories of the Northwoods.

Jean Nicolet
1. ___, a French explorer, is thought to be the first European to see Wisconsin.
2. In 1634 ___ was sent west on an exploratory trip, partly to quiet Indian unrest and partly to gain information about a route to the Pacific. He spent some time in what is now Wisconsin.

Northwest Territory
1. The Northwest Ordinance of 1787 allowed for the creation of 5 states in the northwest portion of the Ohio Valley. These new federal lands were known as the ___.
2. The ___ was eventually organized into the present states of Ohio, Indiana, Illinois, Michigan, and Wisconsin.

Northern Highland
1. Most of northern Wisconsin is in the Northern Highland, which is south of the Lake Superior Lowland.
2. The ___ region is characterized by hundreds of small lakes and heavily forested hills. Timms Hill is in the this region.

Paper
1. The ___ industry in Wisconsin began in 1848 with the opening of a mill to make newsprint for the *Milwaukee Sentinel & Gazette.*
2. Wisconsin is the leading ___-making state by volume, producing more ___ than any state.

Polka
1. The ___ is the official state dance.
2. This dance was chosen because of the state's German heritage.

Red Granite 1. ___ is the state rock. 2. ___ is made mostly of the minerals feldspar and quartz. The reddish feldspars give it its color.	**Song** 1. "On, Wisconsin" is the official state___. 2. In addition to the official state ___, there is also an official waltz and an official ballad. The waltz is "The Wisconsin Waltz," and the ballad is "Oh Wisconsin, Land of My Dreams."
Timms Hill 1. At 1,951 feet above sea level, ___ is the highest point in the state. 2. ___, the highest point in the state, is in the Northern Highland region.	**Tribes** 1. Original Native American ___ of what is now Wisconsin included the Dakota Sioux; the Ho-Chunk, or Winnebago; the Menominee; the Ojibwe, also known as Chippewa, Ojibway, or Ojibwa; the Potawatomi; and the Fox and Sauk. 2. There are 11 federally recognized Native American ___ in the state today.
Union 1. Wisconsin was admitted to the ___ on May 29, 1848. 2. Wisconsin was the 30th state to be admitted to the ___.	**War of 1812** 1. The ___ was conflict between Britain and the U.S. It lasted from 1812 to 1815. 2. The Battle of Prairie du Chien in July 1814 was Wisconsin's only military engagement during the ___.
Western Upland 1. The ___ is west of the Central Plain and Eastern Ridges and Lowland regions. The rugged landscape is mixed with forests and farmland, including many bluffs on the Mississippi River. 2. The ___ region is part of the Driftless Area, which means that it was not covered by glaciers during the most recent ice age.	**Wisconsin River** 1. The ___ runs north-south in the center of the state. Other rivers are the Mississippi, St. Croix, and Chippewa. 2. The ___, a tributary of the Mississippi River, is in the southern portion of the Central Plain.
Wisconsin Territory 1. What is now Wisconsin was part of the Northwest Territory, Indiana Territory, Illinois Territory, Michigan Territory, and ___. 2. ___, created in 1836, included the present-day states of Wisconsin, Minnesota, and Iowa as well as parts of North and South Dakota. Belmont was its first capital. Wisconsin Bingo	**Frank Lloyd Wright** 1. This architect was born in Richland Center, Wisconsin, in 1867. He believed that buildings should reflect and harmonize with their environment. 2. Taliesin, near Spring Green, Wisconsin, was his summer home. © Barbara M. Peller

Wisconsin Bingo

Northern Highland	American Water Spaniel	Joseph Bailey	Lake Michigan	Border (-ed)
Fur Trade	Badger	Wisconsin River	Milk	Red Granite
Western Upland	Marquette and Joliet		Muskellunge	Wisconsin Territory
War of 1812	Polka	Union	Madison	Mississippi River
Mourning Dove	Judicial Branch	Flag	Timms Hill	Lead

Wisconsin Bingo: Card No. 1

Wisconsin Bingo

War of 1812	Western Upland	Lake Winnebago	Paper	Logging
Mississippi River	French and Indian War	Coat of Arms	Polka	Motto
Counties	Judicial Branch		Lake Superior	Union
Jean Nicolet	Northwest Territory	Marquette and Joliet	Frank Lloyd Wright	Border (-ed)
Red Granite	Wisconsin River	Flag	Fur Trade	Timms Hill

Wisconsin Bingo

Judicial Branch	Union	French and Indian War	Madison	Western Upland
Mississippi River	Badger	Crop(s)	American Water Spaniel	Honeybee
Polka	Wisconsin River		Motto	Black Hawk
Marquette and Joliet	Counties	Mourning Dove	Jean Nicolet	Lake Winnebago
Timms Hill	Dairy	Flag	Frank Lloyd Wright	Logging

Wisconsin Bingo: Card No. 3

© Barbara M. Peller

Wisconsin Bingo

Marquette and Joliet	Motto	Joseph Bailey	Dairy	Logging
Milwaukee	Climate	American Water Spaniel	Paper	Western Upland
Muskellunge	Jean Nicolet		Lead	Lake Michigan
Union	Badger	Wisconsin River	Flag	Coat of Arms
Eastern Ridges and Lowlands	Red Granite	Central Plain	Timms Hill	Wisconsin Territory

Wisconsin Bingo: Card No. 4

Wisconsin Bingo

Red Granite	Border (-ed)	Polka	Coat of Arms	Dairy
Milwaukee	Union	Crop(s)	Lake Superior	Badger
Joseph Bailey	Wisconsin Territory		Milk	Green Bay
Lead	Logging	Northern Highland	Frank Lloyd Wright	Executive Branch
French and Indian War	Flag	Western Upland	Marquette and Joliet	Muskellunge

Wisconsin Bingo

Black Hawk	Motto	Lake Winnebago	Logging	Wisconsin Territory
Madison	Polka	Executive Branch	American Water Spaniel	Western Upland
Paper	Eastern Ridges and Lowlands		Climate	Lake Superior
Flag	Mourning Dove	Frank Lloyd Wright	Central Plain	Joseph Bailey
Mississippi River	Coat of Arms	Northern Highland	Muskellunge	Fruit

Wisconsin Bingo

Northern Highland	Motto	Green Bay	Union	French and Indian War
Mississippi River	Logging	Judicial Branch	Badger	Milwaukee
Wisconsin Territory	Lake Michigan		Lake Superior	Climate
Marquette and Joliet	Jean Nicolet	Crop(s)	War of 1812	Counties
Flag	Dairy	Frank Lloyd Wright	Central Plain	Black Hawk

Wisconsin Bingo

Muskellunge	Motto	Galena	Madison	Climate
Milwaukee	Joseph Bailey	Paper	Wisconsin Territory	Coat of Arms
Fruit	Dairy		Logging	Border (-ed)
Timms Hill	Marquette and Joliet	War of 1812	Eastern Ridges and Lowlands	Jean Nicolet
Wisconsin River	Flag	Central Plain	Polka	Mississippi River

Wisconsin Bingo

Lake Superior	French and Indian War	Judicial Branch	Fruit	Dairy
Eastern Ridges and Lowlands	Logging	Muskellunge	Polka	Motto
Honeybee	Northern Highland		Badger	Galena
Executive Branch	Border (-ed)	Mourning Dove	Milk	Green Bay
Jean Nicolet	Frank Lloyd Wright	Crop(s)	War of 1812	Lead

Wisconsin Bingo

War of 1812	Madison	Climate	Paper	Fruit
Wisconsin Territory	Coat of Arms	American Water Spaniel	Badger	Logging
Dairy	Motto		Lake Michigan	Counties
Mourning Dove	Lead	Executive Branch	Frank Lloyd Wright	Honeybee
Crop(s)	Mississippi River	Lake Winnebago	Red Granite	Muskellunge

Wisconsin Bingo

Black Hawk	Motto	Polka	Executive Branch	Mississippi River
Galena	Honeybee	Milk	Lake Superior	American Water Spaniel
Milwaukee	Logging		Lake Winnebago	Judicial Branch
Crop(s)	Western Upland	Frank Lloyd Wright	Dairy	War of 1812
Eastern Ridges and Lowlands	Flag	Northern Highland	Central Plain	French and Indian War

Wisconsin Bingo: Card No. 11

Wisconsin Bingo

French and Indian War	Border (-ed)	Honeybee	Madison	Lake Superior
Judicial Branch	Mississippi River	Joseph Bailey	Central Plain	Badger
Northern Highland	Green Bay		Wisconsin Territory	Paper
Flag	Jean Nicolet	Logging	War of 1812	Milwaukee
Motto	Galena	Dairy	Eastern Ridges and Lowlands	Coat of Arms

Wisconsin Bingo

Executive Branch	Border (-ed)	Black Hawk	Honeybee	Wisconsin Territory
Joseph Bailey	Galena	Logging	Lake Superior	Counties
Madison	Coat of Arms		Judicial Branch	Green Bay
Muskellunge	Frank Lloyd Wright	Climate	Dairy	War of 1812
Flag	Lead	Central Plain	Northern Highland	Milk

Wisconsin Bingo

Fur Trade	Logging	Polka	Lake Superior	Eastern Ridges and Lowlands
Coat of Arms	Northern Highland	Honeybee	Badger	Motto
Executive Branch	Lake Michigan		Lake Winnebago	Crop(s)
Lead	Frank Lloyd Wright	Dairy	Climate	Black Hawk
Flag	Paper	Counties	Mississippi River	Muskellunge

Wisconsin Bingo: Card No. 14

Wisconsin Bingo

Milk	Lake Superior	Polka	French and Indian War	Madison
Black Hawk	Lake Winnebago	American Water Spaniel	Joseph Bailey	Eastern Ridges and Lowlands
Wisconsin Territory	Northern Highland		Western Upland	Motto
Flag	Honeybee	Galena	Frank Lloyd Wright	Executive Branch
Mississippi River	Jean Nicolet	Central Plain	Fruit	Judicial Branch

Wisconsin Bingo: Card No. 15

Wisconsin Bingo

Climate	Honeybee	Galena	Fruit	Northwest Territory
Paper	Counties	Green Bay	Milwaukee	Lake Michigan
Executive Branch	Border (-ed)		Wisconsin Territory	Judicial Branch
Marquette and Joliet	Coat of Arms	Flag	Milk	War of 1812
Eastern Ridges and Lowlands	Tribes	Central Plain	Jean Nicolet	Motto

Wisconsin Bingo

Crop(s)	Song	Legislative Branch	Honeybee	Fur Trade
Milk	Eastern Ridges and Lowlands	Frank Lloyd Wright	Lake Michigan	Green Bay
Lake Superior	Muskellunge		Tribes	Galena
Lead	Mississippi River	War of 1812	Polka	Counties
Mourning Dove	Executive Branch	French and Indian War	Madison	Border (-ed)

Wisconsin Bingo

Fruit	Dairy	Coat of Arms	Executive Branch	Paper
Motto	Crop(s)	Mourning Dove	Wisconsin Territory	Eastern Ridges and Lowlands
Lake Superior	Counties		Legislative Branch	Joseph Bailey
Border (-ed)	American Water Spaniel	Frank Lloyd Wright	War of 1812	Lake Winnebago
Tribes	Honeybee	Polka	Song	Black Hawk

Wisconsin Bingo

Wisconsin Territory	Black Hawk	Honeybee	Galena	War of 1812
Milk	Madison	Motto	French and Indian War	Lake Michigan
Song	Dairy		Badger	Western Upland
Lake Winnebago	Tribes	Mourning Dove	Jean Nicolet	Legislative Branch
Joseph Bailey	Northwest Territory	Mississippi River	Muskellunge	Central Plain

Wisconsin Bingo: Card No. 19

Wisconsin Bingo

Fur Trade	Song	Madison	Honeybee	Central Plain
Coat of Arms	Judicial Branch	Milwaukee	Mourning Dove	Paper
Border (-ed)	Green Bay		Marquette and Joliet	American Water Spaniel
Red Granite	Wisconsin River	Timms Hill	Jean Nicolet	Tribes
Union	Muskellunge	Northwest Territory	War of 1812	Legislative Branch

Wisconsin Bingo: Card No. 20

Wisconsin Bingo

Milk	Black Hawk	Milwaukee	Honeybee	Red Granite
Border (-ed)	Legislative Branch	Climate	Galena	Northern Highland
Counties	Mississippi River		Song	Polka
Mourning Dove	French and Indian War	Tribes	Lead	Muskellunge
Marquette and Joliet	Northwest Territory	Central Plain	Crop(s)	Jean Nicolet

Wisconsin Bingo: Card No. 21

Wisconsin Bingo

Fruit	Lake Winnebago	Legislative Branch	Joseph Bailey	Executive Branch
Paper	Madison	Western Upland	Galena	Badger
Coat of Arms	Lake Michigan		Northern Highland	Green Bay
Tribes	Lead	Jean Nicolet	American Water Spaniel	Milwaukee
Northwest Territory	Crop(s)	Song	Counties	Marquette and Joliet

Wisconsin Bingo

Climate	Song	French and Indian War	Joseph Bailey	Central Plain
Black Hawk	Fur Trade	Mississippi River	Milk	American Water Spaniel
Lake Winnebago	Executive Branch		Timms Hill	Northern Highland
Counties	Northwest Territory	Tribes	Crop(s)	Jean Nicolet
Red Granite	Wisconsin River	Muskellunge	Mourning Dove	Legislative Branch

Wisconsin
Bingo

Central Plain	Ducks, better	French and Indian War	Bear	Glaciers
American Water Spaniel	Milk	Mississippi River	Fur Trade	Black Bear
Northern Highland	Thane Hill		Executive Branch	Lake Winnebago
Jean Nicolet	Crop(s)	Tribes	Northwest Territory	Counter
Legislative Branch	Mourning Dove	Muskellunge	Wisconsin River	Red Granite

Wisconsin Bingo

Climate	Muskellunge	Fur Trade	Song	Galena
Legislative Branch	Central Plain	Milwaukee	Paper	Northern Highland
Green Bay	Fruit		Executive Branch	Counties
Red Granite	Timms Hill	Tribes	Crop(s)	Border (-ed)
Union	Marquette and Joliet	Northwest Territory	Madison	Wisconsin River

Wisconsin Bingo

Marquette and Joliet	Milwaukee	Song	Polka	Legislative Branch
American Water Spaniel	Border (-ed)	Milk	Climate	Badger
Lead	Galena		Timms Hill	Tribes
Western Upland	Red Granite	Wisconsin River	Northwest Territory	Lake Michigan
Central Plain	Fur Trade	Coat of Arms	Eastern Ridges and Lowlands	Union

Wisconsin Bingo

Legislative Branch	Song	Lake Winnebago	Paper	Fruit
Mourning Dove	Madison	Galena	Fur Trade	Climate
Lead	Timms Hill		Lake Michigan	Marquette and Joliet
Crop(s)	Joseph Bailey	Red Granite	Northwest Territory	Tribes
Green Bay	Eastern Ridges and Lowlands	Polka	Wisconsin River	Union

Wisconsin Bingo

Lake Winnebago	Coat of Arms	Song	Fur Trade	Judicial Branch
Red Granite	Timms Hill	Milk	Tribes	Badger
Frank Lloyd Wright	Wisconsin River		Northwest Territory	Marquette and Joliet
Fruit	Black Hawk	Milwaukee	Union	American Water Spaniel
Eastern Ridges and Lowlands	Lake Michigan	Legislative Branch	Western Upland	Green Bay

Wisconsin Bingo: Card No. 27

Wisconsin Bingo

Lake Winnebago	Fur Trade	Western Upland	Song	Climate
Judicial Branch	Legislative Branch	Timms Hill	Paper	Lake Michigan
Wisconsin River	Counties		Green Bay	Mourning Dove
War of 1812	Fruit	Mississippi River	Northwest Territory	Tribes
Joseph Bailey	Lake Superior	Eastern Ridges and Lowlands	Union	Red Granite

Wisconsin Bingo

Legislative Branch	Fur Trade	Fruit	Milk	Lake Superior
Jean Nicolet	Mourning Dove	Milwaukee	Green Bay	Western Upland
Lead	Timms Hill		Badger	Song
Judicial Branch	Red Granite	Logging	Northwest Territory	Tribes
Climate	Galena	Union	Black Hawk	Wisconsin River

Wisconsin Bingo: Card No. 29

Wisconsin Bingo

Dairy	Song	Paper	Lake Superior	Tribes
American Water Spaniel	Fur Trade	Lake Winnebago	Lake Michigan	Badger
Lead	Executive Branch		Green Bay	Milwaukee
Union	Black Hawk	Joseph Bailey	Northwest Territory	Timms Hill
Red Granite	Wisconsin Territory	Wisconsin River	Legislative Branch	Western Upland

Wisconsin Bingo: Card No. 30

www.ingramcontent.com/pod-product-compliance
Lightning Source LLC
LaVergne TN
LVHW061339060426

835511LV00014B/2016